Pasta Carbonara Recipes

A Delectable Collection of Classic and Creative Pasta Carbonara Dishes

While every precaution has been taken in the preparation of this book, the publisher assumes no responsibility for errors or omissions, or for damages resulting from the use of the information contained herein.

PASTA CARBONARA RECIPES

First edition. November 20, 2023.

ISBN: 979-8223460619

Written by john ahmad.

Table of Contents

John Ahmad

Chapter 1: Introduction to Pasta Carbonara

The Origins and History

Pasta Carbonara, a beloved Italian dish, boasts a rich history that's as captivating as its flavor. This chapter delves into the origins and evolution of this classic recipe, tracing its roots back to the heart of Rome.

Origins of Pasta Carbonara

The precise origin of Pasta Carbonara remains a subject of debate, but there are a few popular theories about its creation. One suggests that it was inspired by Roman charcoal workers who mixed eggs and Pecorino Romano cheese with pancetta to create a hearty meal. Another theory ties its inception to Italian coal miners in the mid-20th century. Regardless of its exact origin, Pasta Carbonara has become an emblematic dish of Roman cuisine.

As the story goes, the name "carbonara" is derived from the Italian word "carbone," meaning coal. This connection further supports the theory that the dish was popularized by the coal workers who needed a sustaining and flavorful meal.

Evolution of the Recipe

Over the years, Pasta Carbonara has undergone various transformations. From its humble beginnings as a rustic, working-class dish, it has ascended the culinary ranks to grace the menus of gourmet restaurants worldwide. Chefs have experimented with different pasta shapes, ingredients, and techniques, leading to an array of innovative Carbonara variations.

As the dish gained popularity, its essence remained intact while new ingredients were incorporated to create unique twists. Today, you'll find variations that include everything from seafood and vegetables to unconventional ingredients like truffle oil and foie gras.

Mastering the Perfect Carbonara

Achieving the perfect balance of flavors and textures in a Pasta Carbonara requires a keen understanding of the cooking process. This section offers step-by-step guidance to help you master the art of creating a creamy, delectable Carbonara dish.

Essential Ingredients

Pasta: The choice of pasta plays a significant role in the final dish. While spaghetti is the classic choice, other pasta types like fettuccine, rigatoni, or bucatini can also work wonderfully. Cook the pasta to a perfect al dente texture to ensure a satisfying bite.

Eggs: Eggs are the foundation of the creamy sauce that coats the pasta. The challenge lies in creating a luscious sauce without scrambling the eggs. Whisking them thoroughly and tempering with pasta water are key techniques.

Cheese: Pecorino Romano cheese brings its distinctive salty and nutty flavor to the dish. Grate it fresh to enhance the sauce's richness and depth.

Guanciale or Pancetta: These Italian cured meats provide the dish's characteristic smoky and savory notes. Guanciale, made from pork jowl, offers a more robust flavor, while pancetta, made from pork belly, has a milder taste. Properly sautéing them is crucial to achieving the desired texture and taste.

Cooking Techniques

Sautéing Guanciale/Pancetta: Begin by sautéing thin strips of guanciale or pancetta until they turn golden and crispy. This step imparts the essential smokiness and texture to the dish.

Creating the Sauce: To create the luscious sauce, whisk eggs and grated Pecorino Romano cheese in a bowl. The challenge here is to combine the mixture with the pasta without curdling the eggs. Adding pasta water gradually while tossing prevents the sauce from becoming too thick or scrambled.

Avoiding Common Mistakes: Carbonara has a few potential pitfalls, such as curdled sauce or scrambled eggs. Keeping the heat low and adding pasta water gradually while stirring continuously will help you avoid these issues.

Perfecting Flavor and Texture

Balancing Saltiness: Both the cheese and the cured meat contribute saltiness to the dish. Taste as you go and adjust the amount of salt accordingly to achieve a harmonious balance.

Creamy vs. Dry Carbonara: Carbonara purists often prefer a creamy texture, while some enjoy a drier version with less sauce. Adjust the ratio of eggs and cheese to achieve the consistency you desire.

Putting It All Together

Now that you understand the fundamentals, it's time to put them into practice. Follow this step-by-step recipe to create a delicious Pasta Carbonara that embodies the essence of this classic dish. From boiling the pasta to tossing it in the rich sauce, each detail is carefully outlined to ensure a flawless preparation process.

Chapter 2: Traditional Pasta Carbonara

The Classic Roman Recipe

Embark on a journey to discover the timeless flavors of the original Pasta Carbonara. This chapter unveils the cherished recipe that has captured the hearts and palates of generations, hailing directly from the streets of Rome.

Ingredients:

- 12 ounces (340g) spaghetti
- 4 ounces (113g) guanciale or pancetta, diced
- 2 large eggs
- 1 cup (100g) Pecorino Romano cheese, grated
- Freshly ground black pepper, to taste
- Salt, to taste
- 2 tablespoons olive oil
- 2 cloves garlic, peeled (optional, for flavoring)

Instructions:

1. Bring a large pot of salted water to a boil. Add the spaghetti and cook until al dente. Reserve about 1 cup of pasta cooking water before draining.
2. In a separate bowl, whisk the eggs, grated Pecorino Romano cheese, and a generous amount of freshly ground black pepper. Set aside.
3. In a skillet, heat the olive oil over medium heat. Add the diced guanciale or pancetta and cook until it becomes crispy and golden brown. If desired, add the peeled garlic cloves for a subtle infusion of flavor. Once cooked, remove the garlic cloves

and discard.

4. When the pasta is cooked, quickly transfer it to the skillet with the guanciale or pancetta. Toss to coat the pasta in the rendered fat.

5. Remove the skillet from heat and let it cool slightly (to avoid curdling the eggs). Gradually pour the egg and cheese mixture over the pasta, tossing continuously to create a creamy, glossy sauce. If needed, add a splash of reserved pasta water to achieve the desired consistency.

6. Season with additional black pepper to taste. Taste for saltiness, keeping in mind that the guanciale or pancetta and Pecorino Romano cheese are naturally salty.

7. Serve immediately, garnished with extra grated Pecorino Romano cheese and a sprinkle of black pepper.

Mastering the Basics: Technique and Ingredients

Choosing the Right Pasta: Opt for long and thin pasta varieties like spaghetti or linguine. Their shape allows the sauce to cling and coat evenly.

Eggs and Cheese: Whisk the eggs and cheese until well combined. The heat from the pasta will gently cook the eggs, creating a creamy sauce. Use freshly grated Pecorino Romano for authentic flavor.

Rendered Meat: Sauté the guanciale or pancetta until crispy. This step imparts smokiness and depth to the dish. Use the rendered fat to coat the pasta and create a base for the sauce.

Tempering Eggs: To avoid curdling, allow the pasta and rendered meat to cool slightly before adding the egg and cheese mixture. Toss continuously while adding the mixture gradually.

Creamy Consistency: Achieve a creamy sauce by incorporating pasta water as needed. This helps bind the ingredients and prevents the sauce from becoming too thick.

Flavor Enhancement: The optional addition of garlic cloves to the rendered meat infuses subtle flavor. Remove the garlic before adding the pasta.

Balancing Salt: Be mindful of the saltiness from the guanciale or pancetta and cheese. Taste as you go and adjust the seasoning accordingly.

Mastering the basics of this classic recipe sets the foundation for exploring a world of Pasta Carbonara variations. As you perfect this traditional dish, you'll gain the confidence to experiment with innovative ingredients and techniques in the chapters ahead.

Chapter 3: Spaghetti Variations

Dive into the world of creativity with two unique spins on the classic Pasta Carbonara. These variations incorporate diverse ingredients to elevate your Carbonara experience.

Creamy Mushroom Carbonara

Ingredients:

- 12 ounces (340g) spaghetti
- 8 ounces (227g) mushrooms, sliced
- 4 ounces (113g) pancetta or bacon, diced
- 2 large eggs
- 1 cup (100g) Pecorino Romano cheese, grated
- Freshly ground black pepper, to taste
- Salt, to taste
- 2 tablespoons butter
- 2 cloves garlic, minced
- Fresh parsley, chopped (for garnish)

Instructions:

1. Cook the spaghetti in a pot of salted boiling water until al dente. Reserve 1 cup of pasta cooking water before draining.
2. In a bowl, whisk the eggs, grated Pecorino Romano cheese, and black pepper. Set aside.
3. In a skillet, melt the butter over medium heat. Add the diced pancetta or bacon and cook until crispy. Remove from the skillet and set aside.
4. In the same skillet, add the sliced mushrooms and minced garlic. Sauté until the mushrooms are tender and any moisture has evaporated.

5. Return the cooked pancetta or bacon to the skillet. Toss the mushroom mixture to combine.
6. Remove the skillet from heat and allow it to cool slightly. Add the drained spaghetti and toss to coat with the mushroom and bacon mixture.
7. Gradually pour the egg and cheese mixture over the pasta, tossing continuously to create a creamy sauce. If needed, add reserved pasta water to achieve the desired consistency.
8. Taste for seasoning and adjust with salt and pepper as necessary.
9. Serve immediately, garnished with chopped fresh parsley.

Zucchini and Bacon Delight
Ingredients:

- 12 ounces (340g) spaghetti
- 2 medium zucchinis, julienned
- 4 ounces (113g) bacon, diced
- 2 large eggs
- 1 cup (100g) Pecorino Romano cheese, grated
- Freshly ground black pepper, to taste
- Salt, to taste
- 2 tablespoons olive oil
- 1 teaspoon lemon zest (optional)
- Fresh basil, chiffonade (for garnish)

Instructions:

1. Cook the spaghetti in salted boiling water until al dente. Reserve 1 cup of pasta cooking water before draining.
2. In a bowl, whisk the eggs, grated Pecorino Romano cheese, and black pepper. Set aside.
3. In a skillet, heat the olive oil over medium heat. Add the diced bacon and cook until crispy. Remove from the skillet and set aside.
4. In the same skillet, add the julienned zucchinis. Sauté until they are tender and slightly caramelized.
5. Return the cooked bacon to the skillet with the zucchinis. Toss to combine.
6. Remove the skillet from heat and let it cool slightly. Add the drained spaghetti and toss to mix the ingredients.

1. Gradually pour the egg and cheese mixture over the pasta, tossing continuously to create a creamy sauce. If needed, add

reserved pasta water to achieve the desired consistency.

2. If using, sprinkle lemon zest over the pasta for a refreshing twist.
3. Taste for seasoning and adjust with salt and pepper.
4. Serve immediately, garnished with chiffonade of fresh basil.

Chapter 4: Twists on Tradition

Expand your culinary horizons with inventive interpretations of the classic Pasta Carbonara. These twists infuse new dimensions of flavor while paying homage to the beloved original.

Carbonara-Stuffed Ravioli

Ingredients:

- 24 store-bought ravioli
- 4 ounces (113g) guanciale or pancetta, diced
- 2 large eggs
- 1 cup (100g) Pecorino Romano cheese, grated
- Freshly ground black pepper, to taste
- Salt, to taste
- 2 tablespoons olive oil
- 2 cloves garlic, minced
- Fresh parsley, chopped (for garnish)

Instructions:

1. Cook the ravioli in salted boiling water until they float to the surface. Remove with a slotted spoon and set aside.
2. In a bowl, whisk the eggs, grated Pecorino Romano cheese, and black pepper. Set aside.

1. In a skillet, heat the olive oil over medium heat. Add the diced guanciale or pancetta and cook until crispy. Remove from the skillet and set aside.
2. In the same skillet, add the minced garlic and sauté until fragrant. Remove from heat.
3. In a large mixing bowl, combine the cooked guanciale or pancetta, sautéed garlic, and the egg and cheese mixture. Mix thoroughly.

4. To assemble, carefully stuff each ravioli with a spoonful of the carbonara filling. Press the edges to seal.
5. In the same skillet, heat a bit of olive oil over medium heat. Add the stuffed ravioli and cook until they are lightly browned and heated through.
6. Serve the carbonara-stuffed ravioli garnished with chopped fresh parsley.

Carbonara Pizza

Ingredients:

- 1 prepared pizza dough (store-bought or homemade)
- 4 ounces (113g) guanciale or pancetta, diced
- 2 large eggs
- 1 cup (100g) Pecorino Romano cheese, grated
- Freshly ground black pepper, to taste
- Salt, to taste
- 1 tablespoon olive oil
- 1 cup shredded mozzarella cheese
- Fresh parsley, chopped (for garnish)

Instructions:

1. Preheat your oven according to the pizza dough package instructions or your homemade dough recipe.
2. In a bowl, whisk the eggs, grated Pecorino Romano cheese, and black pepper. Set aside.
3. In a skillet, heat the olive oil over medium heat. Add the diced guanciale or pancetta and cook until crispy. Remove from the skillet and set aside.
4. Roll out the pizza dough on a baking sheet or pizza stone.
5. Spread the egg and cheese mixture evenly over the pizza dough, leaving a border around the edges.
6. Sprinkle the cooked guanciale or pancetta over the egg and cheese mixture.
7. Top the pizza with shredded mozzarella cheese.
8. Bake the pizza in the preheated oven until the crust is golden and the cheese is melted and bubbly.
9. Remove from the oven and let the pizza cool slightly before slicing.
10. Garnish with chopped fresh parsley before serving.

Chapter 5: International Flavors

Embark on a global culinary adventure as we fuse Pasta Carbonara with diverse cultural influences. Explore the delightful marriage of flavors from Thailand and Mexico.

Thai-Inspired Carbonara

Ingredients:

- 12 ounces (340g) spaghetti
- 4 ounces (113g) cooked and peeled shrimp, tails removed
- 2 large eggs
- 1 cup (100g) Pecorino Romano cheese, grated
- Freshly ground black pepper, to taste
- Salt, to taste
- 2 tablespoons vegetable oil
- 1 tablespoon Thai red curry paste
- 1 cup coconut milk
- Fresh cilantro, chopped (for garnish)
- Lime wedges (for serving)

Instructions:

1. Cook the spaghetti in salted boiling water until al dente. Reserve 1 cup of pasta cooking water before draining.
2. In a bowl, whisk the eggs, grated Pecorino Romano cheese, and black pepper. Set aside.
3. In a skillet, heat the vegetable oil over medium heat. Add the Thai red curry paste and sauté for a minute until fragrant.
4. Pour in the coconut milk and bring to a gentle simmer.
5. Add the cooked shrimp to the skillet and cook until they are heated through.

6. Reduce the heat to low and remove the skillet from the stove. Allow it to cool slightly before adding the drained spaghetti. Toss to combine.

7. Gradually pour the egg and cheese mixture over the pasta, tossing continuously to create a creamy sauce. If needed, add reserved pasta water to achieve the desired consistency

8. Taste for seasoning and adjust with salt and pepper.

9. Serve immediately, garnished with chopped fresh cilantro and lime wedges on the side.

Mexican Carbonara Quesadillas

Ingredients:

- 8 small flour tortillas
- 4 ounces (113g) chorizo sausage, casing removed and crumbled
- 2 large eggs
- 1 cup (100g) Pecorino Romano cheese, grated
- Freshly ground black pepper, to taste
- Salt, to taste
- 1 cup shredded Monterey Jack cheese
- 1/2 cup diced tomatoes
- 1/4 cup chopped fresh cilantro
- Sour cream and salsa (for serving)

Instructions:

1. In a skillet, cook the crumbled chorizo over medium heat until browned and cooked through. Remove from the skillet and set aside.
2. In a bowl, whisk the eggs, grated Pecorino Romano cheese, and black pepper. Set aside.
3. Lay out four tortillas on a flat surface. Sprinkle shredded Monterey Jack cheese over each tortilla.
4. Divide the cooked chorizo among the tortillas.
5. Pour the egg and cheese mixture evenly over the chorizo on each tortilla.
6. Top with diced tomatoes and chopped cilantro.
7. Place the remaining four tortillas over the toppings to create quesadillas.
8. In a clean skillet, cook each quesadilla over medium heat until the cheese is melted and the tortilla is golden brown on both sides.
9. Slice the quesadillas into wedges and serve with sour cream and

salsa on the side.

Chapter 6: Seafood Delights

Delve into the ocean's bounty as we combine the elegance of seafood with the indulgent allure of Pasta Carbonara. Prepare to savor the exquisite flavors of shrimp, scallops, and lobster.

Shrimp and Scallop Carbonara

Ingredients:

- 12 ounces (340g) spaghetti
- 8 ounces (227g) shrimp, peeled and deveined
- 8 ounces (227g) sea scallops
- 2 large eggs
- 1 cup (100g) Pecorino Romano cheese, grated
- Freshly ground black pepper, to taste
- Salt, to taste
- 2 tablespoons butter
- 2 cloves garlic, minced
- Fresh parsley, chopped (for garnish)
- Lemon wedges (for serving)

Instructions:

1. Cook the spaghetti in salted boiling water until al dente. Reserve 1 cup of pasta cooking water before draining.
2. In a bowl, whisk the eggs, grated Pecorino Romano cheese, and black pepper. Set aside.
3. In a skillet, melt the butter over medium heat. Add the minced garlic and sauté until fragrant.
4. Add the shrimp and scallops to the skillet. Cook until the shrimp turn pink and the scallops are opaque and lightly browned. Remove from the skillet and set aside.

5. In the same skillet, toss the cooked seafood with the drained spaghetti.
6. Remove the skillet from heat and let it cool slightly. Gradually pour the egg and cheese mixture over the pasta and seafood, tossing continuously to create a creamy sauce. If needed, add reserved pasta water to achieve the desired consistency.
7. Taste for seasoning and adjust with salt and pepper.
8. Serve immediately, garnished with chopped fresh parsley and lemon wedges on the side.

Lobster Carbonara Extravaganza
Ingredients:

- 12 ounces (340g) spaghetti
- 8 ounces (227g) cooked lobster meat, chopped
- 2 large eggs
- 1 cup (100g) Pecorino Romano cheese, grated
- Freshly ground black pepper, to taste
- Salt, to taste
- 2 tablespoons butter
- 2 shallots, finely chopped
- 1/4 cup dry white wine
- Fresh chives, chopped (for garnish)

Instructions:

1. Cook the spaghetti in salted boiling water until al dente. Reserve 1 cup of pasta cooking water before draining.
2. In a bowl, whisk the eggs, grated Pecorino Romano cheese, and black pepper. Set aside.
3. In a skillet, melt the butter over medium heat. Add the finely chopped shallots and sauté until translucent.

4. Pour in the dry white wine and simmer until it's reduced by half.
5. Add the chopped lobster meat to the skillet. Toss to coat in the shallot and wine mixture.
6. Remove the skillet from heat and let it cool slightly. Gradually pour the egg and cheese mixture over the pasta and lobster, tossing continuously to create a creamy sauce. If needed, add reserved pasta water to achieve the desired consistency
7. Taste for seasoning and adjust with salt and pepper.
8. Serve immediately, garnished with chopped fresh chives.

Chapter 7: Veggie-Packed Creations

Elevate your Pasta Carbonara experience with the vibrant flavors and textures of vegetables. Discover the perfect harmony between creamy Carbonara and nutritious greens.

Roasted Veggie Carbonara

Ingredients:

- 12 ounces (340g) spaghetti
- 2 cups mixed roasted vegetables (e.g., bell peppers, zucchini, cherry tomatoes)
- 2 large eggs
- 1 cup (100g) Pecorino Romano cheese, grated
- Freshly ground black pepper, to taste
- Salt, to taste
- 2 tablespoons olive oil
- Fresh basil, chopped (for garnish)

Instructions:

1. Cook the spaghetti in salted boiling water until al dente. Reserve 1 cup of pasta cooking water before draining.
2. In a bowl, whisk the eggs, grated Pecorino Romano cheese, and black pepper. Set aside.
3. In a large skillet, heat the olive oil over medium heat. Add the roasted vegetables and sauté briefly to warm them.
4. Toss the drained spaghetti in the skillet with the roasted vegetables.
5. Remove the skillet from heat and let it cool slightly. Gradually pour the egg and cheese mixture over the pasta and vegetables, tossing continuously to create a creamy sauce. If needed, add

reserved pasta water to achieve the desired consistency.

6. Taste for seasoning and adjust with salt and pepper.
7. Serve immediately, garnished with chopped fresh basil.

Spinach and Artichoke Carbonara
Ingredients:

- 12 ounces (340g) spaghetti
- 2 cups baby spinach leaves
- 1 cup canned artichoke hearts, drained and quartered
- 2 large eggs
- 1 cup (100g) Pecorino Romano cheese, grated
- Freshly ground black pepper, to taste
- Salt, to taste
- 2 tablespoons butter
- 2 cloves garlic, minced
- Fresh parsley, chopped (for garnish)

Instructions:

1. Cook the spaghetti in salted boiling water until al dente. Reserve 1 cup of pasta cooking water before draining.
2. In a bowl, whisk the eggs, grated Pecorino Romano cheese, and black pepper. Set aside.
3. In a skillet, melt the butter over medium heat. Add the minced garlic and sauté until fragrant.
4. Add the baby spinach leaves to the skillet. Sauté until wilted.
5. Toss in the quartered artichoke hearts.
6. Remove the skillet from heat and let it cool slightly. Gradually pour the egg and cheese mixture over the pasta and vegetables, tossing continuously to create a creamy sauce. If needed, add reserved pasta water to achieve the desired consistency.
7. Taste for seasoning and adjust with salt and pepper.
8. Serve immediately, garnished with chopped fresh parsley.

Chapter 8: Healthier Alternatives

Indulge in the rich flavors of Pasta Carbonara while embracing healthier choices. Discover how turkey bacon and whole wheat pasta contribute to a more nutritious version of this beloved dish.

Turkey Bacon Carbonara

Ingredients:

- 12 ounces (340g) whole wheat spaghetti
- 4 ounces (113g) turkey bacon, diced
- 2 large eggs
- 1 cup (100g) Pecorino Romano cheese, grated
- Freshly ground black pepper, to taste
- Salt, to taste
- 2 tablespoons olive oil
- Fresh parsley, chopped (for garnish)

Instructions:

1. Cook the whole wheat spaghetti in salted boiling water until al dente. Reserve 1 cup of pasta cooking water before draining.
2. In a bowl, whisk the eggs, grated Pecorino Romano cheese, and black pepper. Set aside.
3. In a skillet, heat the olive oil over medium heat. Add the diced turkey bacon and cook until crispy. Remove from the skillet and set aside.
4. Toss the cooked whole wheat spaghetti in the skillet with the crispy turkey bacon.
5. Remove the skillet from heat and let it cool slightly. Gradually pour the egg and cheese mixture over the pasta and turkey bacon, tossing continuously to create a creamy sauce. If needed, add reserved pasta water to achieve the desired consistency.

6. Taste for seasoning and adjust with salt and pepper.
7. Serve immediately, garnished with chopped fresh parsley.

Whole Wheat Pasta Carbonara
Ingredients:

- 12 ounces (340g) whole wheat spaghetti
- 4 ounces (113g) guanciale or turkey bacon, diced
- 2 large eggs
- 1 cup (100g) Pecorino Romano cheese, grated
- Freshly ground black pepper, to taste
- Salt, to taste
- 2 tablespoons olive oil
- Fresh thyme leaves, for garnish

Instructions:

1. Cook the whole wheat spaghetti in salted boiling water until al dente. Reserve 1 cup of pasta cooking water before draining.
2. In a bowl, whisk the eggs, grated Pecorino Romano cheese, and black pepper. Set aside.
3. In a skillet, heat the olive oil over medium heat. Add the diced guanciale or turkey bacon and cook until crispy. Remove from the skillet and set aside.
4. Toss the cooked whole wheat spaghetti in the skillet with the crispy guanciale or turkey bacon.
5. Remove the skillet from heat and let it cool slightly. Gradually pour the egg and cheese mixture over the pasta and guanciale or turkey bacon, tossing continuously to create a creamy sauce. If needed, add reserved pasta water to achieve the desired consistency.
6. Taste for seasoning and adjust with salt and pepper.
7. Serve immediately, garnished with fresh thyme leaves.

Chapter 9: Decadent Indulgences

Elevate your Pasta Carbonara experience to new heights with opulent ingredients that add a touch of luxury. Delight in the exquisite flavors of truffle oil and foie gras.

Truffle Oil Infusion

Ingredients:

- 12 ounces (340g) spaghetti
- 4 ounces (113g) pancetta or guanciale, diced
- 2 large eggs
- 1 cup (100g) Pecorino Romano cheese, grated
- Freshly ground black pepper, to taste
- Salt, to taste
- 2 tablespoons olive oil
- Truffle oil, for drizzling
- Fresh chives, chopped (for garnish)

Instructions:

1. Cook the spaghetti in salted boiling water until al dente. Reserve 1 cup of pasta cooking water before draining.
2. In a bowl, whisk the eggs, grated Pecorino Romano cheese, and black pepper. Set aside.
3. In a skillet, heat the olive oil over medium heat. Add the diced pancetta or guanciale and cook until crispy. Remove from the skillet and set aside.
4. Toss the cooked spaghetti in the skillet with the crispy pancetta or guanciale.
5. Remove the skillet from heat and let it cool slightly. Gradually pour the egg and cheese mixture over the pasta and pancetta or guanciale, tossing continuously to create a creamy sauce. If

needed, add reserved pasta water to achieve the desired consistency.

6. Taste for seasoning and adjust with salt and pepper.
7. Drizzle truffle oil over the pasta and toss to infuse the luxurious flavor.
8. Serve immediately, garnished with chopped fresh chives.

Carbonara with Foie Gras
Ingredients:

- 12 ounces (340g) spaghetti
- 2 ounces (57g) foie gras, diced
- 2 large eggs
- 1 cup (100g) Pecorino Romano cheese, grated
- Freshly ground black pepper, to taste
- Salt, to taste
- 2 tablespoons butter
- 2 cloves garlic, minced
- Fresh parsley, chopped (for garnish)

Instructions:

1. Cook the spaghetti in salted boiling water until al dente. Reserve 1 cup of pasta cooking water before draining.
2. In a bowl, whisk the eggs, grated Pecorino Romano cheese, and black pepper. Set aside.
3. In a skillet, melt the butter over medium heat. Add the minced garlic and sauté until fragrant.
4. Add the diced foie gras to the skillet. Cook until it's seared and slightly crispy. Remove from the skillet and set aside.
5. Toss the cooked spaghetti in the skillet with the seared foie gras.
6. Remove the skillet from heat and let it cool slightly. Gradually

pour the egg and cheese mixture over the pasta and foie gras, tossing continuously to create a creamy sauce. If needed, add reserved pasta water to achieve the desired consistency.

7. Taste for seasoning and adjust with salt and pepper.
8. Serve immediately, garnished with chopped fresh parsley.

Chapter 10: One-Pot Wonders

Streamline your cooking process with these convenient one-pot variations of Pasta Carbonara. Experience the same rich flavors with a fraction of the cleanup.

Instant Pot Carbonara

Ingredients:

- 12 ounces (340g) spaghetti
- 4 ounces (113g) guanciale or pancetta, diced
- 2 large eggs
- 1 cup (100g) Pecorino Romano cheese, grated
- Freshly ground black pepper, to taste
- Salt, to taste
- 1 tablespoon olive oil
- 3 cups chicken or vegetable broth
- Fresh parsley, chopped (for garnish)

Instructions:

1. Set the Instant Pot to "Sauté" mode. Add the olive oil and diced guanciale or pancetta. Cook until crispy. Remove and set aside.
2. In a bowl, whisk the eggs, grated Pecorino Romano cheese, and black pepper. Set aside.
3. Pour in the chicken or vegetable broth and bring it to a gentle simmer.
4. Break the spaghetti in half and add it to the Instant Pot, ensuring that it's submerged in the broth.
5. Close the Instant Pot lid and set the manual pressure cooking time for half the time recommended on the pasta package.
6. Once the cooking is complete, perform a quick pressure release.
7. Open the Instant Pot lid and switch to "Sauté" mode. Stir in the

cooked guanciale or pancetta.

8. Gradually pour the egg and cheese mixture over the pasta, tossing continuously to create a creamy sauce.

9. Taste for seasoning and adjust with salt and pepper.

10. Serve immediately, garnished with chopped fresh parsley.

Skillet Carbonara
Ingredients:

- 12 ounces (340g) spaghetti
- 4 ounces (113g) pancetta or guanciale, diced
- 2 large eggs
- 1 cup (100g) Pecorino Romano cheese, grated
- Freshly ground black pepper, to taste
- Salt, to taste
- 2 tablespoons olive oil
- 1 cup chicken or vegetable broth
- Fresh parsley, chopped (for garnish)

Instructions:

1. In a large skillet, heat the olive oil over medium heat. Add the diced pancetta or guanciale and cook until crispy. Remove and set aside.
2. In the same skillet, pour in the chicken or vegetable broth and bring to a gentle simmer.
3. Break the spaghetti in half and add it to the skillet, ensuring that it's submerged in the broth.
4. Cook the spaghetti in the broth until it's al dente and most of the liquid has been absorbed.
5. In a bowl, whisk the eggs, grated Pecorino Romano cheese, and black pepper. Set aside.
6. Stir in the cooked pancetta or guanciale.
7. Gradually pour the egg and cheese mixture over the pasta, tossing continuously to create a creamy sauce.
8. Taste for seasoning and adjust with salt and pepper.
9. Serve immediately, garnished with chopped fresh parsley.

Chapter 11: Comfort Food Classics

Experience the nostalgic embrace of comfort food with these hearty adaptations of Pasta Carbonara. Dive into the irresistible allure of Carbonara-infused mac and cheese and tender stuffed meatballs.

Carbonara Mac and Cheese

Ingredients:

- 12 ounces (340g) macaroni or elbow pasta
- 4 ounces (113g) pancetta or guanciale, diced
- 2 large eggs
- 1 cup (100g) Pecorino Romano cheese, grated
- Freshly ground black pepper, to taste
- Salt, to taste
- 2 tablespoons butter
- 2 tablespoons all-purpose flour
- 2 cups milk
- 2 cups shredded cheddar cheese
- Fresh parsley, chopped (for garnish)

Instructions:

1. Cook the macaroni or elbow pasta in salted boiling water until al dente. Reserve 1 cup of pasta cooking water before draining.
2. In a bowl, whisk the eggs, grated Pecorino Romano cheese, and black pepper. Set aside.
3. In a large skillet, melt the butter over medium heat. Add the diced pancetta or guanciale and cook until crispy. Remove and set aside.
4. Add the flour to the skillet and cook for a minute to create a roux.

5. Gradually pour in the milk while whisking continuously to create a smooth sauce.
6. Stir in the shredded cheddar cheese until melted and creamy.
7. Combine the cooked pasta with the cheese sauce.
8. Remove the skillet from heat and let it cool slightly. Gradually pour the egg and cheese mixture over the pasta and sauce, tossing continuously to create a creamy texture. If needed, add reserved pasta water to achieve the desired consistency.
9. Taste for seasoning and adjust with salt and pepper.
10. Serve immediately, garnished with chopped fresh parsley.

Carbonara-Stuffed Meatballs
Ingredients:

- 1 pound (450g) ground beef
- 1/2 pound (225g) ground pork
- 1 cup breadcrumbs
- 2 large eggs
- 1 cup (100g) Pecorino Romano cheese, grated
- Freshly ground black pepper, to taste
- Salt, to taste
- 4 ounces (113g) pancetta or guanciale, diced
- 2 cloves garlic, minced
- Fresh parsley, chopped
- Marinara sauce (for serving)

Instructions:

1. Preheat the oven to 375°F (190°C).
2. In a bowl, combine the ground beef, ground pork, breadcrumbs, eggs, grated Pecorino Romano cheese, black pepper, and salt. Mix until well combined.
3. In a skillet, cook the diced pancetta or guanciale until crispy. Remove and set aside.
4. In the same skillet, sauté the minced garlic until fragrant.
5. Combine the cooked pancetta or guanciale and sautéed garlic with the meat mixture. Add chopped fresh parsley and mix well.
6. Take a portion of the meat mixture and flatten it in your hand. Place a small amount of the carbonara mixture in the center and encase it with the meat, shaping it into a meatball.
7. Repeat the process with the remaining meat and carbonara mixture.
8. Place the stuffed meatballs on a baking sheet and bake in the preheated oven for about 20-25 minutes, or until cooked

through.

9. Serve the stuffed meatballs with marinara sauce and additional grated Pecorino Romano cheese.

Chapter 12: Breakfast and Brunch

Start your day with a delightful twist on Pasta Carbonara. Elevate your morning routine with these breakfast and brunch creations that combine the essence of Carbonara with the comfort of morning fare.

Carbonara Frittata

Ingredients:

- 6 large eggs
- 1/2 cup (50g) Pecorino Romano cheese, grated
- Freshly ground black pepper, to taste
- Salt, to taste
- 4 ounces (113g) pancetta or guanciale, diced
- 1 tablespoon olive oil
- 2 cups baby spinach
- Fresh parsley, chopped (for garnish)

Instructions:

1. Preheat the oven to 350°F (175°C).
2. In a bowl, whisk the eggs, grated Pecorino Romano cheese, black pepper, and salt.
3. In an oven-safe skillet, cook the diced pancetta or guanciale over medium heat until crispy. Remove from the skillet and set aside.
4. In the same skillet, heat the olive oil. Add the baby spinach and sauté until wilted.
5. Spread the cooked pancetta or guanciale evenly in the skillet.
6. Pour the egg and cheese mixture over the pancetta or guanciale and spinach.
7. Cook the frittata on the stovetop over medium heat for a few

minutes until the edges begin to set.

8. Transfer the skillet to the preheated oven and bake for about 10-15 minutes, or until the frittata is set in the center.

9. Remove from the oven and let it cool slightly before slicing.

10. Serve the Carbonara frittata garnished with chopped fresh parsley.

Carbonara Breakfast Burritos
Ingredients:

- 4 large eggs
- 1/4 cup (25g) Pecorino Romano cheese, grated
- Freshly ground black pepper, to taste
- Salt, to taste
- 4 ounces (113g) cooked bacon or sausage, crumbled
- 2 large flour tortillas
- 1/2 cup diced tomatoes
- 1/4 cup chopped fresh parsley
- Hot sauce, for serving (optional)

Instructions:

1. In a bowl, whisk the eggs, grated Pecorino Romano cheese, black pepper, and salt.
2. In a skillet, cook the bacon or sausage until crispy or fully cooked. Remove from the skillet and set aside.
3. In the same skillet, scramble the eggs over medium heat until they are cooked to your desired consistency.
4. Warm the flour tortillas in the skillet or microwave.
5. Lay out each tortilla and divide the scrambled eggs between them.
6. Sprinkle crumbled bacon or sausage over the eggs.
7. Top with diced tomatoes and chopped fresh parsley.
8. Roll up the tortillas into burritos.
9. Serve the Carbonara breakfast burritos with hot sauce on the side, if desired.

Chapter 13: Fusion Fusion

Embark on a culinary adventure that blends Pasta Carbonara with international flavors in unexpected ways. Explore the fusion of Italian and Japanese cuisines with Carbonara Sushi Rolls and savor the harmony of Carbonara and Mexican spices in Carbonara Tacos.

Carbonara Sushi Rolls

Ingredients:

- 2 cups sushi rice, cooked and seasoned
- 2 sheets nori (seaweed)
- 4 ounces (113g) pancetta or guanciale, diced and cooked
- 2 large eggs, scrambled and cooked
- 1/2 cup (50g) Pecorino Romano cheese, grated
- Freshly ground black pepper, to taste
- Salt, to taste
- 1/2 avocado, sliced
- 1/4 cup cream cheese, softened
- Soy sauce, for dipping

Instructions:

1. Lay out a bamboo sushi rolling mat and place a sheet of plastic wrap over it.
2. Place a sheet of nori on the plastic wrap, shiny side down.

1. Wet your hands to prevent sticking, then spread half of the seasoned sushi rice evenly over the nori, leaving about 1 inch of nori on the top edge.
2. Sprinkle grated Pecorino Romano cheese over the rice.
3. Arrange the diced cooked pancetta or guanciale and scrambled

eggs over the cheese.

4. Lay out slices of avocado and spread a thin layer of softened cream cheese over the ingredients.

5. Season with freshly ground black pepper and a pinch of salt.

6. Carefully lift the bamboo mat and start rolling the nori tightly, using the mat to shape the roll.

7. Use a bit of water to seal the top edge of the nori.

8. Once the roll is complete, allow it to rest for a minute before slicing into bite-sized pieces.

9. Serve the Carbonara sushi rolls with soy sauce for dipping.

Carbonara Tacos
Ingredients:

- 8 small flour tortillas
- 8 ounces (227g) cooked and shredded chicken
- 4 ounces (113g) pancetta or guanciale, diced and cooked
- 2 large eggs, scrambled and cooked
- 1/2 cup (50g) Pecorino Romano cheese, grated
- Freshly ground black pepper, to taste
- Salt, to taste
- Sliced red onion, for garnish
- Chopped fresh cilantro, for garnish
- Lime wedges, for serving

Instructions:

1. Warm the flour tortillas according to the package instructions.
2. In a bowl, combine the cooked and shredded chicken, diced cooked pancetta or guanciale, and scrambled eggs.
3. Sprinkle grated Pecorino Romano cheese over the mixture.
4. Season with freshly ground black pepper and a pinch of salt.
5. Divide the Carbonara mixture among the warmed tortillas.
6. Garnish with sliced red onion and chopped fresh cilantro.
7. Serve the Carbonara tacos with lime wedges on the side.

Chapter 14: Quick and Easy Fixes

When time is of the essence, satisfy your Carbonara cravings with these speedy solutions. Discover a 15-minute version that doesn't compromise on flavor and indulge in a Microwave Carbonara for one that's ready in a flash.

15-Minute Carbonara

Ingredients:

- 12 ounces (340g) spaghetti
- 4 ounces (113g) pancetta or guanciale, diced
- 2 large eggs
- 1 cup (100g) Pecorino Romano cheese, grated
- Freshly ground black pepper, to taste
- Salt, to taste
- 2 tablespoons olive oil
- Fresh parsley, chopped (for garnish)

Instructions:

1. Cook the spaghetti in salted boiling water until al dente. Reserve 1 cup of pasta cooking water before draining.
2. In a bowl, whisk the eggs, grated Pecorino Romano cheese, and black pepper. Set aside.
3. In a large skillet, heat the olive oil over medium heat. Add the diced pancetta or guanciale and cook until crispy. Remove from the skillet and set aside.
4. Toss the cooked spaghetti in the skillet with the crispy pancetta or guanciale.
5. Remove the skillet from heat and let it cool slightly. Gradually pour the egg and cheese mixture over the pasta and pancetta

or guanciale, tossing continuously to create a creamy sauce. If needed, add reserved pasta water to achieve the desired consistency.

6. Taste for seasoning and adjust with salt and pepper.
7. Serve immediately, garnished with chopped fresh parsley.

Microwave Carbonara for One

Ingredients:

- 4 ounces (113g) spaghetti
- 2 ounces (57g) pancetta or guanciale, diced
- 1 large egg
- 1/4 cup (25g) Pecorino Romano cheese, grated
- Freshly ground black pepper, to taste
- Salt, to taste
- Fresh parsley, chopped (for garnish)

Instructions:

1. Cook the spaghetti in a microwave-safe bowl with water according to the package instructions. Drain the pasta.
2. In a separate microwave-safe bowl, cook the diced pancetta or guanciale until crispy.
3. In a small bowl, whisk the egg, grated Pecorino Romano cheese, black pepper, and salt.
4. Add the cooked and drained spaghetti to the bowl with the crispy pancetta or guanciale.
5. Gradually pour the egg and cheese mixture over the pasta, tossing continuously to create a creamy sauce.
6. Microwave the pasta for about 30 seconds to warm the sauce slightly.
7. Taste for seasoning and adjust with salt and pepper.

8. Serve immediately, garnished with chopped fresh parsley.

Chapter 15: Rustic and Homemade

Immerse yourself in the authentic charm of Pasta Carbonara with these rustic and homemade interpretations. Craft your own pasta from scratch and relish the flavors of a cozy campfire-inspired Carbonara.

Handmade Pasta Carbonara

Ingredients:

For the Pasta:

- 2 cups all-purpose flour
- 3 large eggs

For the Carbonara:

- Handmade pasta
- 4 ounces (113g) pancetta or guanciale, diced
- 2 large eggs
- 1 cup (100g) Pecorino Romano cheese, grated
- Freshly ground black pepper, to taste
- Salt, to taste
- 2 tablespoons olive oil
- Fresh parsley, chopped (for garnish)

Instructions:

Handmade Pasta:

1. On a clean surface, mound the flour and create a well in the center.
2. Crack the eggs into the well and gently beat them with a fork, gradually incorporating the flour.
3. Once a dough forms, knead it for about 5-7 minutes until

smooth and elastic.

4. Wrap the dough in plastic wrap and let it rest for at least 30 minutes.
5. Roll out the dough and cut it into desired pasta shapes.
6. Cook the handmade pasta in salted boiling water until al dente. Reserve 1 cup of pasta cooking water before draining.

Carbonara:

1. In a bowl, whisk the eggs, grated Pecorino Romano cheese, and black pepper. Set aside.
2. In a large skillet, heat the olive oil over medium heat. Add the diced pancetta or guanciale and cook until crispy. Remove from the skillet and set aside.
3. Toss the cooked handmade pasta in the skillet with the crispy pancetta or guanciale.
4. Remove the skillet from heat and let it cool slightly. Gradually pour the egg and cheese mixture over the pasta and pancetta or guanciale, tossing continuously to create a creamy sauce. If needed, add reserved pasta water to achieve the desired consistency.
5. Taste for seasoning and adjust with salt and pepper.
6. Serve immediately, garnished with chopped fresh parsley.

Backyard Campfire Carbonara
   Ingredients:

- 12 ounces (340g) spaghetti
- 4 ounces (113g) pancetta or guanciale, diced
- 2 large eggs

- 1 cup (100g) Pecorino Romano cheese, grated
- Freshly ground black pepper, to taste
- Salt, to taste
- 2 tablespoons olive oil
- 1/2 cup frozen peas
- 1/4 cup grated Parmesan cheese
- Fresh parsley, chopped (for garnish)

Instructions:

1. Cook the spaghetti in salted boiling water until al dente. Reserve 1 cup of pasta cooking water before draining.
2. In a bowl, whisk the eggs, grated Pecorino Romano cheese, and black pepper. Set aside.
3. In a large skillet, heat the olive oil over a campfire or portable stove. Add the diced pancetta or guanciale and cook until crispy. Remove from the skillet and set aside.
4. Toss the cooked spaghetti in the skillet with the crispy pancetta or guanciale.
5. Add the frozen peas to the skillet and cook until heated through.
6. Remove the skillet from heat and let it cool slightly. Gradually pour the egg and cheese mixture over the pasta, tossing continuously to create a creamy sauce. If needed, add reserved pasta water to achieve the desired consistency
7. Sprinkle grated Parmesan cheese over the pasta and toss to combine.
8. Taste for seasoning and adjust with salt and pepper.
9. Serve immediately, garnished with chopped fresh parsley.

Chapter 16: Elegant Dinner Party Delights

Impress your guests with sophisticated twists on Pasta Carbonara that elevate your dinner party to a memorable occasion. Delight in mini Carbonara tartlets and savor the exquisite flavors of Carbonara-stuffed chicken breast.

Mini Carbonara Tartlets

Ingredients:

For the Tartlet Shells:

- 1 sheet puff pastry, thawed
- Flour, for dusting

For the Carbonara Filling:

- 4 ounces (113g) pancetta or guanciale, diced and cooked
- 2 large eggs
- 1 cup (100g) Pecorino Romano cheese, grated
- Freshly ground black pepper, to taste
- Salt, to taste
- 1/4 cup heavy cream
- Fresh chives, chopped (for garnish)

Instructions:

Tartlet Shells:

1. Preheat the oven to 375°F (190°C).
2. Roll out the puff pastry on a floured surface and cut out small rounds to fit your mini tartlet pans.
3. Press the pastry rounds into the tartlet pans and prick the

bottoms with a fork.

4. Bake the tartlet shells for about 10-15 minutes, or until golden brown and puffed.

Carbonara Filling:

1. In a bowl, whisk the eggs, grated Pecorino Romano cheese, black pepper, and salt. Set aside.
2. In a separate bowl, whisk the heavy cream.
3. Mix the diced cooked pancetta or guanciale with the egg and cheese mixture.
4. Gradually add the heavy cream, stirring to combine and create a creamy filling.

Assembling:

1. Carefully spoon the Carbonara filling into the baked tartlet shells.
2. Garnish with chopped fresh chives.
3. Serve the mini Carbonara tartlets as elegant appetizers.

Carbonara-stuffed Chicken Breast
Ingredients:

- 4 boneless, skinless chicken breasts
- Salt and freshly ground black pepper, to taste
- 4 ounces (113g) pancetta or guanciale, diced and cooked
- 2 large eggs
- 1 cup (100g) Pecorino Romano cheese, grated
- Freshly ground black pepper, to taste
- 1/4 cup heavy cream
- Fresh parsley, chopped (for garnish)

Instructions:

1. Preheat the oven to 375°F (190°C).
2. Carefully butterfly each chicken breast to create a pocket for stuffing.
3. In a bowl, whisk the eggs, grated Pecorino Romano cheese, black pepper, and salt. Set aside.
4. In a separate bowl, whisk the heavy cream.
5. Mix the diced cooked pancetta or guanciale with the egg and cheese mixture.
6. Gradually add the heavy cream, stirring to combine and create a creamy filling.
7. Spoon the Carbonara filling into the pocket of each chicken breast.
8. Secure the openings with toothpicks.
9. Season the outside of the chicken breasts with salt and pepper.
10. Place the stuffed chicken breasts in a baking dish and bake for about 25-30 minutes, or until the chicken is cooked through.
11. Remove the toothpicks before serving.
12. Garnish with chopped fresh parsley

Chapter 17: Side Dishes and Accompaniments

Complete your Pasta Carbonara experience with these delectable side dishes and accompaniments that complement the flavors and elevate your meal to perfection.

Garlic Bread Carbonara Toasts

Ingredients:

- Baguette or French bread, sliced
- Butter, softened
- Garlic cloves, minced
- 4 ounces (113g) pancetta or guanciale, diced and cooked
- 1 cup (100g) Pecorino Romano cheese, grated
- Freshly ground black pepper, to taste
- Salt, to taste
- Fresh parsley, chopped (for garnish)

Instructions:

1. Preheat the oven to 375°F (190°C).
2. In a bowl, mix softened butter with minced garlic to create a garlic butter spread.
3. Spread the garlic butter generously on the sliced baguette or French bread.
4. Toast the bread slices in the preheated oven for about 5-7 minutes, or until golden brown and crisp.
5. In a bowl, mix the diced cooked pancetta or guanciale with the grated Pecorino Romano cheese.
6. Season the mixture with freshly ground black pepper and a pinch of salt.
7. Carefully spoon the Carbonara mixture onto the toasted bread

slices.

8. Return the toasts to the oven for an additional 2-3 minutes, or until the cheese is melted and bubbly.
9. Garnish with chopped fresh parsley.
10. Serve the Garlic Bread Carbonara Toasts as a delightful side or appetizer.

Carbonara Caesar Salad
Ingredients:
For the Dressing:

- 1/4 cup mayonnaise
- 1/4 cup grated Pecorino Romano cheese
- 1 tablespoon Dijon mustard
- 2 garlic cloves, minced
- 2 tablespoons lemon juice
- Salt and freshly ground black pepper, to taste

For the Salad:

- Romaine lettuce, chopped
- Croutons
- Grated Pecorino Romano cheese
- 4 ounces (113g) pancetta or guanciale, diced and cooked
- Freshly ground black pepper, to taste

Instructions:
Dressing:

1. In a bowl, whisk together mayonnaise, grated Pecorino Romano cheese, Dijon mustard, minced garlic, and lemon juice.
2. Season the dressing with salt and freshly ground black pepper.

3. Adjust the consistency with a splash of water if needed.

Salad:

1. In a large bowl, combine the chopped Romaine lettuce and croutons.
2. Toss the salad with the Carbonara dressing until well coated.
3. Sprinkle grated Pecorino Romano cheese over the salad.
4. Add the diced cooked pancetta or guanciale.
5. Season with freshly ground black pepper.
6. Toss the salad gently to combine all the flavors.
7. Serve the Carbonara Caesar Salad as a refreshing and indulgent side dish.

Chapter 18: Cooking for a Crowd

Host a culinary feast with ease as you cater to a crowd. These crowd-pleasing dishes—Giant Carbonara Potluck Casserole and Carbonara Pasta Bar—will ensure everyone enjoys the Pasta Carbonara experience together.

Giant Carbonara Potluck Casserole

Ingredients:

- 1 pound (450g) spaghetti
- 8 ounces (227g) pancetta or guanciale, diced and cooked
- 8 large eggs
- 2 cups (200g) Pecorino Romano cheese, grated
- Freshly ground black pepper, to taste
- Salt, to taste
- 1 cup heavy cream
- Fresh parsley, chopped (for garnish)

Instructions:

1. Preheat the oven to 375°F (190°C).
2. Cook the spaghetti in salted boiling water until slightly undercooked. Reserve 1 cup of pasta cooking water before draining.
3. In a large bowl, whisk the eggs, grated Pecorino Romano cheese, black pepper, and salt. Set aside.
4. In another bowl, whisk the heavy cream.
5. Mix the diced cooked pancetta or guanciale with the egg and cheese mixture.

6. Gradually add the heavy cream, stirring to combine and create a creamy sauce

7. Toss the slightly undercooked spaghetti in the Carbonara mixture.

8. If needed, add reserved pasta water to achieve the desired consistency.

9. Transfer the Carbonara mixture to a large baking dish.

10. Bake in the preheated oven for about 20-25 minutes, or until the casserole is set and golden on top.

11. Garnish with chopped fresh parsley.

12. Serve the Giant Carbonara Potluck Casserole to a delighted crowd.

Carbonara Pasta Bar
Ingredients:
For the Carbonara Base:

- 2 pounds (900g) spaghetti
- 16 ounces (454g) pancetta or guanciale, diced and cooked
- 12 large eggs
- 3 cups (300g) Pecorino Romano cheese, grated
- Freshly ground black pepper, to taste
- Salt, to taste
- 1 1/2 cups heavy cream

For the Toppings:

- Sauteed mushrooms
- Roasted cherry tomatoes
- Sautéed spinach
- Grated Parmesan cheese
- Red pepper flakes
- Chopped fresh herbs (parsley, basil, chives, etc.)

Instructions:
Carbonara Base:

1. Cook the spaghetti in salted boiling water until al dente. Reserve 2 cups of pasta cooking water before draining.
2. In a large bowl, whisk the eggs, grated Pecorino Romano cheese, black pepper, and salt. Set aside.
3. In another bowl, whisk the heavy cream.
4. Mix the diced cooked pancetta or guanciale with the egg and cheese mixture.
5. Gradually add the heavy cream, stirring to combine and create a creamy sauce.
6. Toss the cooked spaghetti in the Carbonara mixture.
7. If needed, add reserved pasta water to achieve the desired consistency.

Carbonara Pasta Bar:

1. Set up a pasta bar with the Carbonara base and various toppings.
2. Guests can customize their Carbonara bowls with sautéed mushrooms, roasted cherry tomatoes, sautéed spinach, grated Parmesan cheese, red pepper flakes, and chopped fresh herbs.
3. Provide tongs and serving utensils for guests to create their personalized Carbonara masterpieces.
4. Encourage guests to experiment with different combinations of toppings.
5. Enjoy the interactive Carbonara Pasta Bar experience as a lively crowd-pleaser.

Chapter 19: Sweet Endings

Conclude your Pasta Carbonara journey on a sweet note with these indulgent and imaginative desserts. Delight your taste buds with the delicate flavors of Carbonara-inspired dessert crepes and the unique allure of candied bacon and egg gelato.

Carbonara-Inspired Dessert Crepes

Ingredients:

For the Crepes:

- 1 cup all-purpose flour
- 2 large eggs
- 1 1/2 cups milk
- 2 tablespoons melted butter
- Pinch of salt

For the Filling:

- 1/2 cup mascarpone cheese
- 1/4 cup Nutella or chocolate hazelnut spread
- Fresh strawberries, sliced
- Powdered sugar, for dusting

Instructions:

Crepes:

1. In a bowl, whisk together the flour, eggs, milk, melted butter, and a pinch of salt until smooth.
2. Heat a non-stick skillet over medium heat. Pour a small amount of batter into the skillet, swirling to coat the bottom evenly.
3. Cook the crepe for about 1-2 minutes on each side, until lightly

golden. Repeat with the remaining batter.

Filling:

1. In a bowl, mix the mascarpone cheese and Nutella until well combined.

Assembling:

1. Lay out a crepe and spread a generous spoonful of the mascarpone-Nutella mixture in the center.
2. Add a few slices of fresh strawberries on top.
3. Fold the sides of the crepe over the filling to create a triangular shape.
4. Dust the crepe with powdered sugar.
5. Repeat with the remaining crepes and filling.
6. Serve the Carbonara-Inspired Dessert Crepes for a delightful and sweet finale.

Candied Bacon and Egg Gelato
Ingredients:

- 2 cups whole milk
- 1 cup heavy cream
- 3/4 cup granulated sugar
- Pinch of salt
- 4 large egg yolks
- 1 teaspoon vanilla extract
- 4 ounces (113g) candied bacon, chopped
- Dark chocolate shavings, for garnish

Instructions:

1. In a saucepan, heat the whole milk, heavy cream, granulated sugar, and a pinch of salt over medium heat. Stir until the sugar is dissolved and the mixture is heated.
2. In a separate bowl, whisk the egg yolks.
3. Gradually pour the hot milk mixture into the egg yolks, whisking continuously.
4. Return the mixture to the saucepan and cook over low heat, stirring constantly, until it thickens and coats the back of a spoon.
5. Remove from heat and stir in the vanilla extract.
6. Allow the mixture to cool, then refrigerate until chilled.
7. Churn the cooled mixture in an ice cream maker according to the manufacturer's instructions.
8. During the last few minutes of churning, add the chopped candied bacon to the ice cream.
9. Transfer the gelato to a lidded container and freeze until firm.
10. Serve the Candied Bacon and Egg Gelato in bowls, garnished with dark chocolate shavings.

Chapter 20: Tips, Tricks, and Garnishes

Become a Pasta Carbonara maestro with these expert tips, tricks, and innovative garnishes. Elevate your Carbonara creations to new heights with creamy texture perfection and imaginative finishing touches.

Perfecting Creamy Texture

Timing is Key: To achieve a creamy Carbonara sauce, remove the pan from heat before adding the egg and cheese mixture. The residual heat will cook the eggs gently without curdling.

Reserved Pasta Water: Save a cup of pasta cooking water before draining. Adding a splash of pasta water to your Carbonara helps create a silky, luscious sauce by emulsifying the egg and cheese mixture.

Toss Like a Pro: Toss the cooked pasta with the sauce off the heat. This allows the sauce to cling to the pasta evenly, resulting in a luxurious texture.

Balancing Act: Balance the richness with acidity. A squeeze of fresh lemon juice can brighten the flavors and cut through the richness of the sauce.

Creative Carbonara Garnishes

Fresh Herbs: Elevate your Carbonara with a sprinkle of freshly chopped herbs like parsley, basil, chives, or thyme. Their vibrant flavors add depth and color.

Microgreens: Delicate microgreens, such as arugula, watercress, or micro basil, make for a visually appealing and flavorful garnish.

Citrus Zest: Add a burst of freshness with citrus zest. Lemon or orange zest can provide a zingy contrast to the richness of Carbonara.

Cracked Black Pepper: Give a final flourish with a generous crack of freshly ground black pepper. The aromatic spice adds complexity and a hint of heat.

Crispy Prosciutto: Swap out traditional pancetta or guanciale for crispy prosciutto bits. Their salty crunch complements the creamy pasta.

Toasted Nuts: Think beyond meat and add texture with toasted nuts like pine nuts, chopped walnuts, or almonds. They bring a satisfying crunch.

Cheese Variations: Experiment with different cheese blends. Try adding grated Parmesan, Asiago, or a touch of blue cheese for a unique twist.

Poached Egg: Top your Carbonara with a perfectly poached egg. The runny yolk adds a luxurious and velvety element to each bite.

Truffle Essence: Elevate the dish to gourmet status by drizzling truffle oil or adding shaved truffle for an indulgent aroma and earthy flavor.

Edible Flowers: Impress with edible flowers like nasturtiums, pansies, or violets. They add a delicate touch and a touch of whimsy.

In conclusion, "Pasta Carbonara Recipes" is a comprehensive and creative cookbook that celebrates the beloved Italian dish, Pasta Carbonara, in all its glorious forms. From traditional recipes to innovative twists, from breakfast to dessert, this cookbook offers a wide range of options to satisfy every palate and occasion.

As you embark on your culinary journey through these pages, you'll explore the origins and history of Pasta Carbonara, master the techniques to achieve the perfect creamy texture, and discover tips and tricks to elevate your Carbonara creations to new heights.

With chapters dedicated to various variations, including vegetarian options, international flavors, seafood delights, comfort food classics, and even sweet endings, you'll find something for every taste and dietary preference. The cookbook takes you step by step through each recipe, providing detailed instructions and ingredient lists to ensure your success in the kitchen.

Whether you're cooking for a cozy dinner at home, hosting a vibrant dinner party, or simply looking for creative ways to enjoy Pasta Carbonara, this cookbook has you covered. Each recipe is thoughtfully crafted to bring out the rich and savory flavors that make Carbonara a cherished favorite.

As you explore the pages of "Pasta Carbonara Recipes," you'll not only enhance your cooking skills but also create memorable experiences for yourself and your loved ones. The versatility of Pasta Carbonara, as showcased in this cookbook, is a testament to the endless possibilities that can emerge from a single dish.

So, gather your ingredients, sharpen your culinary skills, and immerse yourself in the world of Pasta Carbonara. From classic renditions to innovative fusions, this cookbook is your passport to a culinary adventure that will delight and inspire. May your kitchen be filled with the aroma of sizzling pancetta, freshly grated cheese, and the joy of creating a masterpiece that's both comforting and elegant.

Happy cooking, and bon appétit!